J. R. L. Anderson

The Discovery of America

With illustrations by
Graham Humphreys

Puffin Books

Explorer 7

Contents

Puffin Books: a Division of Penguin Books Ltd, Harmondsworth, Middlesex, England
Penguin Books Inc., 7110 Ambassador Road, Baltimore, Maryland 21207, U.S.A.
Penguin Books Australia Ltd, Ringwood, Victoria, Australia
First published 1973
Text copyright © J. R. L. Anderson 1973
Illustrations copyright © Penguin Books Ltd 1973
Made and printed in Great Britain by W. S. Cowell Ltd, Butter Market, Ipswich

A Very Long Time Ago

If you look up the word 'discovery' in a dictionary you will see it described as 'finding out'. What the word alone can't tell you is, whose finding out? When I was about ten I landed from a rowing boat onto a little island in a river. I had never been there before, I had not known that the island existed: did I discover it? Well, yes, I did. My island had been known to other people for centuries, but as far as I was concerned I came upon it for the first time, and for me it was a discovery. So when we talk of 'discovering' America, or anywhere else, we want to be clear about what we mean.

We who live in long-established countries, with long histories of all the things that men and women of our nation have done in the world, tend to be rather arrogant about other people's discoveries. We say that Christopher Columbus 'discovered' America; but what of all the people he found living there already? Had not they, or their many-times great-grandparents, discovered America long ago? What we mean is that Columbus found a land that his own people – directly, the Italians and Spaniards, more generally, the inhabitants of Western Europe – had not known about before. And even that is not really true, for there were people in other parts of Western Europe, even in England, who knew something of America long before Columbus sailed in 1492. Yet in another sense Columbus *did* discover America – just as I discovered my island. Nothing much happened as a result of my discovery, but the consequences that flowed from the voyages of Columbus were vastly important to all the rest of the world, and that is why Columbus is in the history books, and my little voyage is not. So there are two quite separate things to think about – discovery, or the finding out of places by people who did not *themselves* know about them before, and what happened as a result of these discoveries. In this book we shall try to keep both these aspects of discovery clearly in our minds, and we shall see that the discovery of America is not something that just happened at some moment of time, but is part of a continuing process that has been going on for many tens of thousands of years. There are particularly exciting chapters in the story, but the whole story is really much more exciting than any of its chapters.

Europe, Asia and Africa are called the Old World, North and South America, the New. This came about partly because people living in the Old World wrote the books, but the names contain an important truth : human life seems to have begun in what is called the Old World. The miracle of evolution took place in Asia or Africa, possibly at different times in both. If you read it as an allegory or simple folktale, the story of Adam and Eve (though maybe there should be three or four Adams and Eves in widely scattered parts of the Old World continents) is not so far from the truth of how man came into being and of how his children went out to populate the earth.

No one knows precisely where Adam and Eve had their first home, but it was not in America. People who study the bones and structure of men and try to work out the origins of mankind are called anthropologists. They have found that the American Indians – why they are called Indians we shall come to later – are related to the Mongolian peoples of Asia, one of the great families of mankind. They are not very closely related, for they left their original family group a very long time ago, but they are definitely related. If you

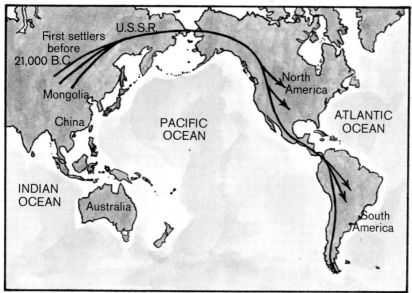

Early immigration routes.

look at a map or a globe, you will see that Asia and North America are not far apart. Alaska, in North America, is separated from the north-easterly tip of Asia only by a narrow stretch of sea called the Bering Strait. This was not always sea, and once it was possible to walk across it, either over land, before the sea broke through, or, in the ice ages, by a kind of ice-bridge. The first people in America, the discoverers of the New World for mankind, walked there from Asia across the Bering Strait, then (though it had no name) more properly called the Bering Isthmus, or part-isthmus, part-ice-bridge. They made their journey at some time before about 21,000 B.C., perhaps some thousands of years before.

Twenty to thirty thousand years ago – how can we begin to feel the meaning of such a span of time ? It is best to think of it simply as a very long time ago, remembering always, however, that what is long in our time-scale is still momentary in terms of the age of rocks and geological time, measured not in thousands but in hundreds of millions of years.

So the first men reached America from Asia before 21,000 B.C. But there were no records kept then, because nobody could write. How do we know even the roughest sort of date?

Anthropology is a kind of detective story; there are no written records by early man, but there are clues in his own bones, in the stone tools he made, in what can be worked out about the physical conditions in which he lived. An interesting clue to the arrival of the first Americans is in their Mongolian relationship. The American Indian tends to have the high cheekbones and some other characteristics of his distant Mongolian ancestors, but he does *not* have the flat face, slit eyes and other features of the now-typical Mongolian of northern Asia, or of his near cousin, the Eskimo of the Arctic. Anthropologists have worked out that these particular Mongolian characteristics were developed by evolution as a protection against extreme cold. Now round about 21,000 B.C. the world entered one of its so-called 'ice ages'

A present-day American Indian and a Mongolian of northern Asia.

(it lasted until about 11,000 B.C.) and the climate of northern Asia became extremely cold. It is thought that the people living in northern Asia developed their particular anti-cold characteristics during those ten thousand years, from 21,000 to about 11,000 B.C. A distinguished anthropologist, Professor William Howells, of Harvard University, has suggested that the early Americans were more closely related to an *older* Mongolian stock, and crossed to America *before* the Mongolians who went on living in Asia developed all the features that we regard as typically Mongolian today. This means that the first Americans must have crossed before 21,000 B.C.* This can only be a theory, but it fits the known facts, for example that between 21,000 B.C. and 11,000 B.C. ice was so thick over the whole area of the Bering Strait that it is doubtful if anyone could have lived in the region, let alone travelled over it.

After 11,000 B.C. migration again became possible, and it made little difference when the sea broke through the Bering Isthmus to form the Bering Strait. Men living on those Arctic coasts early became expert in the use of kayaks, and in those days there was a fairly constant coming and going of peoples between Asia and North America – the Canadian and Greenland Eskimoes, for instance, are newcomers compared with the American Indians. Doubtless other Asiatics, instead of staying in the Arctic, followed their forbears into continental America after 11,000 B.C. to add to the stock that gradually populated the whole continent from Alaska to Tierra del Fuego at the very tip of South America. But the evidence suggests that the first Americans came before 21,000 B.C. and put their own stamp on the New World that opened before them as they spread south and east from their points of arrival on the north Pacific coast.

These first arrivals brought little with them, a few chipped stones that would cut after a fashion and help to skin an animal, a stick or two, and that was about all. Early man was a hunter and food-gatherer, living on what he could pick up – shellfish, if he lived near a beach, roots and berries

* The recent discovery (1973) of a very old human skull in South America seems to confirm this early date.

The first crossing into North America over the then Bering Isthmus.

where he could find them – and on such animals as he could
kill. He had no settled home, and with his small family group
he wandered constantly – he had to as he used up whatever
he could find to eat. Mostly he wandered backwards and
forwards over a known stretch of territory, which he regarded, and fought to defend, as his family or tribal hunting
ground. Every generation or so, however, some individual
would be born, more curious and bolder than his fellows,
who would go farther afield, to see what he might come to.
This exploring instinct in man is as old as man himself, and
it helped the human race to survive by finding new lands to
live in, new animals to hunt, new kinds of things to eat. Most
of those who first crossed from Asia to America probably

wandered back again, or lived out their short lives on the
Alaskan coast. But some, with the exploring instinct more
strongly in them, ventured inland, or journeyed on along
the coast. Many of them must have died before they got far,
but those who survived did well, for, although they did not
know it, a whole continent lay before them, theirs for the
taking, and with a more favourable climate as they travelled
south. Over the next 15,000 years or so they peopled it – it
is reckoned that man got to the islands round Cape Horn,
at the southern tip of South America, by about 8,000 B.C.
Man then was still a fairly rare creature in the New World,
and the vast area of the two Americas was thinly peopled.
But by about 10,000 years ago early forms of human ways of

life were all established from the Arctic to the jungles of the Amazon, from the great plains of North America to the pampas of Argentina.

It is not known when, or how, agriculture came to the New World. Here we must touch upon a problem which will occupy us a good deal as we go on : were the major inventions of mankind, the bow and arrow, the planting of food crops, spinning and weaving, and a host of other skills, devised and developed independently in many different parts of the world, or were they once-for-all inventions in one place, with the knowledge of them slowly spread by the wanderings of men themselves ? It is common enough for two or more people to have the same ideas at different times ; the idea of the bow, for instance, using the spring of a sapling to propel another stick, might occur to an ingenious boy any-

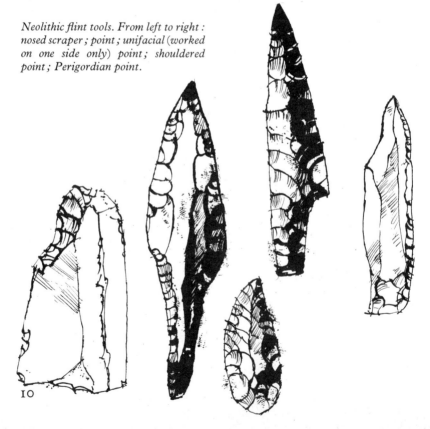

Neolithic flint tools. From left to right :
nosed scraper ; point ; unifacial (worked
on one side only) point ; shouldered
point ; Perigordian point.

where. An observant man or woman anywhere might notice that plants grow from a seed, and experiment by planting the seed of some fruit that he or she particularly liked. But it is less easy to accept that such complex skills as spinning and weaving – simple enough when you are shown how to do them, but hard to work out for oneself – were all invented again and again by lots of different people. The biggest change in human history was brought about by what is called the Neolithic Revolution, which seems to have started in the Middle East round about ten thousand years ago. 'Neolithic' comes from two Greek words, and means 'New Stone'. It is used to describe one of the ages of mankind – the New Stone Age, characterized by the use of sharper and better flint tools than those of the Palaeolithic (Old Stone) Age. But Neolithic, although it has been in the language too long to be changed, is a bad name for an immensely important period, for it was not better flint-working, useful as it was, that really changed human life, but the invention of farming, which came about at roughly the same time. Instead of having to depend for food on what he could find or hunt, man discovered that he could plant crops and grow what he wanted. Even more important, he found that he could grow more than he needed for himself and his family. This made it possible for men with special skills – healers of the sick, carvers of wood or bone, men who could make music from reeds, men who could tell stories – to devote themselves fulltime to their arts, living on the food that other men produced in return for practising their skills. Whether the early Americans invented agriculture independently, or whether the idea was carried to them by some new wave of immigrants from Asia, or by explorers who came by sea, no one can say. But the farming revolution came to the New World as to the Old, and the descendants of the first discoverers of America were able to create some wonderful civilizations of their own. How much they created for themselves, and how much – if anything – they learned from other explorers, we shall consider in the next chapter.

A Long Time Ago

There are odd references to the New World in ancient Old
World writings, but what any of them really mean is hard
to say. The Greek philosopher Plato (429–347 B.C.) tells the
story of Atlantis, a legendary land with an advanced civilization which was supposed to have been swallowed up in some
great flood, which formed the Atlantic Ocean. There is no
physical evidence that any large land-mass can ever have
existed in the Atlantic, at least in the remotest of historical
times, and modern theory inclines to the view that Plato's
story embodies folk-memories of a volcanic explosion in the
eastern Mediterranean which blew up the island of Santo-
rini and destroyed the ancient civilization of Crete (around
1,500 B.C.). Nevertheless, the very existence of the Atlantis
legend prompts puzzling questions. Why was it even
imagined that this mysterious land was in the Atlantic (or
where the Atlantic now is)? To the ancient world the sea
beyond the Pillars of Hercules (the Straits of Gibraltar) was
not merely unknown – you were supposed to fall off the edge
of the world if you ventured on it. Yet here is a writer in the
fourth century B.C. peopling it with a mysterious civilization.
Science fiction a couple of thousand years ago? Or does the
Atlantis legend embody some vague knowledge of the existence of the American continent?

It is not impossible. History has tended to be written by
land-based scholars, more familiar with the study than the
sea. Everything that comes to light about ancient seafaring
carries it farther and farther back in time: the sea has always
been a highway as well as a barrier, and rafts or small boats
have been making long voyages since man discovered that a
log of wood will float. The ancient Greeks themselves, the
Phoenicians, and the Carthaginians were all great seafarers.

As far back as 600 B.C. a Phoenician fleet was chartered by the Egyptian Pharaoh, Necho, and commissioned to sail round Africa. The voyage is recorded by the Greek historian Herodotus (fifth century B.C.), who says that it took two-and-a-half years and adds a number of details which suggest that it really took place. Of particular interest in considering the spread of early ideas on agriculture is his statement that every autumn the voyagers would put in at some convenient spot on the coast, sow a patch of ground, and wait for next year's harvest before sailing on. This practical means of securing fresh rations for a voyage would bring new crops for the local inhabitants to study.

By the middle of the fifth century B.C. the Carthaginians had rounded Cape Verde and sailed far down the coast of West Africa – one such voyage, made about 450 B.C. under

Ra II in mid-Atlantic.

13

a commander called Hanno, is recorded. Probably there were unrecorded voyages long before that. From West Africa to the Caribbean, and on to Central and South America is not a difficult route, and boats may be helped by ocean currents and the prevailing winds. The late Sir Francis Chichester (1901–72) chose this part of the Atlantic (from Portuguese Guinea to Nicaragua) for his successful attempt in 1971 to establish new speed records for sustained single-handed sailing. Thor Heyerdahl, the Norwegian scientist and explorer, is convinced that seafarers of the ancient world did cross from North Africa to America in reed boats, and in 1969–70 he made two transatlantic voyages in reed boats to prove that it could be done. Heyerdahl found another reed boat link between South America and the ancient world : he found that Indians living by Lake Titicaca on the borders of Peru and Bolivia constructed reed boats on precisely the same lines as those illustrated in tomb pictures from ancient Egypt.

Evidence of contact by sea between the Old World and the New far back in time is strong. Cotton cloth was woven in South and Central America long before the coming of Columbus and the Spaniards at the end of the fifteenth century A.D., yet American wild cotton has too short a fibre to be of any use for spinning or weaving. The cotton grown and woven in America for the past 2000 years or more is a mixed plant that can have come into existence only by crossing the cotton seed with some other variety of cotton seed from the Old World. Moreover, the looms used by the ancient inhabitants of Peru were remarkably similar to those used in ancient Egypt. Cotton is one of the most telling of the silent witnesses to early contact with the Americas, but there are other plants, among them the bottle gourd and a certain kind of bean, which tell the same story. Seeds, of course, can get into the sea and be carried long distances by ocean currents without the help of man, but it is too much to suppose that all these strange transplantings, particularly the crossbreeding of cotton, came about by chance.

There are other things. The ancient peoples of America created several remarkable civilizations, the best known of which are the Mayan and Aztec civilizations of Guatemala, Mexico and Central America, and the Inca and pre-Inca cultures of Peru and Ecuador. Earlier than the Mayan civilization in Central America is a more shadowy culture – but yet one that reached a high order of civilization – known as the Olmec. These great civilizations have curious links with those of Mesopotamia and ancient Egypt, and they came later in time, which at least suggests that their development may have been helped by ideas brought from the Old World. The Aztec and the Inca civilizations were destroyed by the Spaniards in the sixteenth century A.D. The Mayan flourished earlier, in the first centuries of the Christian era, and there were pre-Inca cultures long before the Inca civilization that the Spaniards found. The Olmec peoples were forerunners of the Maya.

The Mayan pyramid at Chichen Itza.

These Olmec-Mayan peoples, from as far back as several centuries B.C., built stone pyramids much on the lines of the Egyptian pyramids, and practised the art of mummifying the dead. They had an extraordinarily advanced knowledge of mathematics and astronomy. Their calendar, based on a year of 365·242 days, was slightly more accurate than our own. They had a pictographic writing, and – mathematically of extraordinary interest – they had a figure for zero, or nil, a concept that Europe did not have until it was learned from Arab mathematicians quite late in historical time during the Middle Ages.

Those who argue against the possibility of early contacts between America and the Old World point to many things that the early American civilizations did *not* have. They knew nothing of iron, and went on using mostly stone tools, making sharp and efficient knives from a particularly hard form of rock called obsidian. They did not have, or apparently did not use, the wheel. If there had been contact with the Old World, it is argued, is it possible that travellers would not have brought with them knowledge of all these useful things?

These are certainly matters to be weighed in the evidence, but they do not weigh all that much. Metallic iron is not found free in nature anywhere in the Americas, except for a very little round the Great Lakes in Canada, where some Indian tribes did make a little use of it. It is not easy to make a furnace hot enough to smelt iron from ore, and there were advanced civilizations in the Old World which knew little or nothing of iron. Other forms of metal working were well developed in the Americas long before Columbus sailed. The Central American civilizations, and the Inca and pre-Inca cultures of Ecuador and Peru, all produced fine work in gold and silver and copper and the peoples of Ecuador and Peru knew how to mix tin with copper to make bronze. Their goldsmiths cast beautiful statuettes and ornaments by covering a wax pattern with clay and then firing, or baking the clay, so that the wax would melt, leaving a hollow mould of the desired shape inside the baked clay. This is technically known as the 'lost wax' process, and is identical with the process used by craftsmen in the ancient civilizations of the Middle East and Mediterranean.

There was a prehistoric horse in America – indeed, the horse as we have always known it is said to have evolved from this prehistoric prototype which crossed into Asia when there was still land across the Bering Strait. But the breed became extinct in the American continent and horses were not known again anywhere in America until they were reintroduced by the Spaniards. There were no draught animals in America in this early period: the native Andean llama is quite good for carrying packs, but not for pulling carts. Men, of course, can lighten their own labour by using wheelbarrows or trolleys for moving heavy goods. The wheel was not developed by the early Americans, but it was not unknown, for little wheeled toys have been found by archaeologists.

Wheeled toy deer or dog, from Central Vera Cruz.

17

Evidence that people from the Old World *did* cross the Atlantic to reach Central and South America at various times during the past 2,000–3,000 years is strong. The similarities of technology and culture are too many for them all to be put down to the chance of independent invention, and the folk myths that tell of bearded strangers coming from the sea, bringing skills and knowledge with them, almost certainly have substance. More direct evidence of contact by sea very early in human history has come to light with the discovery in Ecuador of pottery dating back to around 3,000 B.C. which is remarkably similar both in design and texture to pottery made a little earlier in Japan. If ocean voyages at this great distance in time seem incredible, remember that remote islands in the Pacific were all populated somehow, by voyages of deliberate exploration, or by men and women in little boats fleeing from invasion, or simply blown off-course by chance. The survival value of even a tiny boat with a crew who know how to handle her is high; and primitive people, accustomed to going hungry, lived more simply than we do, and could survive physical hardships that most of us could not.

Some people feel that *real* history begins only with writing, but things were happening in the world long before men learned to write. Without a written record, a document of some sort or an inscription carved on stone, we can seldom know *exactly* how or when things took place, but study of the tools, pottery and household goods that ancient peoples had buried with them, or left behind when they moved on somewhere else (archaeology), and of the fossilized remains of bones and plants (palaeontology), can build up a fairly accurate picture of what must have happened in the past. It is like a detective story, with one clue leading to another until there is a convincing chain of evidence pointing to an inescapable conclusion. Of course it is always possible to doubt some piece of evidence and it may be necessary to say 'this is *probably* what happened', but where there are very many clues, all pointing to the same conclusion, it becomes a reasonable certainty. Thor Heyerdahl has listed some sixty close similarities in technology, habits and practices between the peoples of Central and South America and the civilizations of the Old World, and when the botanical evidence of plants which must have been *brought* to the American continent is added, the case for saying that seafarers of antiquity *must* have landed there becomes overwhelmingly strong. The geographical pattern of ancient civilizations in America bears this out. The great civilizations, that grew up in America before Columbus, were all in Central America or the north-western parts of South America. The Caribbean coast of Central America is the natural journey's end for trade-wind voyages from North Africa or Spain, and you can fairly easily sail between Central America and the north-west of South America along the Pacific coast. Archaeological and cultural evidence from the Pacific shows what immense voyages were possible in early times. Our early voyagers from the Mediterranean world, the Phoenicians, Carthaginians or Greeks, will have sailed from the Atlantic coast of Morocco, been driven across the Atlantic by the weather, or by sheer adventure, and landed

The Atlantic trade winds.

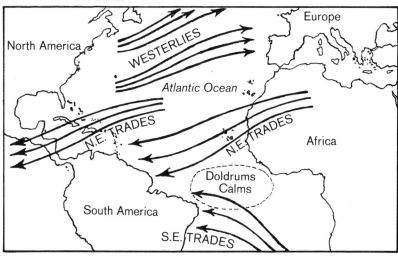

Overleaf: A Phoenician trader.

somewhere in what are now Mexico, Guatemala, Honduras or Nicaragua, probably having put in for water and fresh food at one or other of the West Indian islands on the way. We cannot say *when* these voyages were made; we can, I think, say that they *were* made. Did any of these old explorers ever get back home ? Again, we cannot say, but the Atlantis legend and other odd references in ancient writings to possible Atlantic lands suggest that some dim knowledge of the New World did exist in the Old World between 2,000–3,000 years ago. If so, why was this knowledge lost ? Well, it may not have been *wholly* lost, but changed into legend and myth. Successful voyages in the ancient world, particularly if they brought back gold or silver, were usually closely-guarded secrets, with deliberately false sailing directions so that no one else could go the same way. Only the ship's master and perhaps his mate would know much about navigation, and they would keep quiet about it ; their sailors would tell tall stories, which would not be believed. As the countries of Western Europe developed there was plenty of scope for merchants, without risking money on sending ships to look for fanciful lands across the ocean. And the evidence points to voyages *from* the Old World *to* the New, not the other way. One suspects that over the centuries *some* voyagers did get back, but it is not likely that many did. For the most part these were voyages of no return, their survivors either perishing in trying to get home, or living out the rest of their lives as strange beings able to teach strange skills to the peoples they had come to.

But because the New World learned some of its skills from the Old, it does not follow that ancient American civilizations were not also independently American. Let us think of a modern example, say, locomotion. The steam locomotive was invented in England, the automobile in Germany and France, the aeroplane in the United States. But railways, motor cars and aeroplanes were soon in use all over the world, ingenious men in a hundred different lands all contributing to their improvement.

Irish Monks and Vikings

We come now to history and what may be called nearly-history, the written records of voyages that were undoubtedly made, although just where they got to may remain uncertain. The first record of an authentic voyage which *may* have reached the West Indies, the American mainland, or both, is that of the Irish monk Saint Brendan, who set sail towards the end of the sixth century A.D., some time around 570. Brendan was certainly a real person, and he lived at a time when the Irish church felt a special mission to establish monasteries or hermit's cells in lonely places; and did establish such religious communities in the Orkneys, the Shetlands, the Faeroe Islands, and far-away Iceland. Those Irish monks had two great assets – remarkably seaworthy boats, and the kind of courage that came from the simplicity of their faith that they were doing God's work and, if they perished, could expect to go to Heaven.

The Irish *curragh*, still in use on the west coast of Ireland, and similar to the coracle still used by fishermen in some of the estuaries of Wales, is built of skins (nowadays more often specially-treated canvas) on a wicker frame. It is light, strong, and immensely seaworthy, and it can be rowed or sailed. After making a number of *curragh* voyages to the Hebrides and Brittany, St Brendan set off with fourteen companions to seek a 'promised land' lying somewhere far across the Atlantic. After calling at the Faeroes they sailed and drifted for three months (fasting every other day, as no doubt they often had to) until they came to an island which may reasonably be identified with Madeira. Then they sailed on, apparently met the weed-covered Sargasso Sea, from which they escaped by rowing, and finally reached other

St Brendan and his companions in their little Irish curragh.

islands, which may have included the Bahamas and Jamaica. After many more adventures they did reach their 'promised land', which they explored for forty days, and concluded that it was so big that it must be a continent rather than an island. This must have been somewhere on the eastern seaboard of North America; no other location is possible – the land had a kindly climate and was certainly neither the Arctic nor tropical West Africa.

Set out like this, St Brendan's voyage is wholly credible. Unfortunately, it is not set out like this. The voyage can only be deduced from clues and topographical descriptions in medieval manuscripts, which have attracted the devoted work of generations of scholars. St Brendan left no log. For some three centuries stories of him were handed on by word of mouth, getting much mixed up in the telling. The first written account we have of his Atlantic adventures is in a medieval manuscript called *Navigatio Sancti Brendani* (*The Voyage of St Brendan*), composed about the year 870. Can we believe it?

It is first of all a religious work, full of miracles and divine intervention to help the voyagers, and it must be seen as far as possible through medieval eyes, in which the sight of fishes rising on the sea to hear St Brendan say Mass is a 'fact' at least as real as, and considerably more important than, the description of some landfall. To us, the whole thing is more like a sort of religious fairy story. But even fairy stories have a setting, and the setting of St Brendan's adventures can be based only on real knowledge of Atlantic seas and coasts. There is too much realistic description for it all to be put down to monkish imagination. *Somebody* experienced the weeds of the Sargasso, the fogs off Newfoundland or New England, the fruit and bright colours of the West Indies and all the other geographical facts which make the setting for the miracles. We cannot be sure that that somebody was St Brendan, but since the voyage is traditionally his, it seems more likely than not that the experiences, or at least some of them, were his, and his companions'. It is more likely still that the written account of his voyage, which was written some three centuries after it took place, contains the experiences of several voyages, some made by St Brendan, others by men who followed him. What can be accepted as a reasonable certainty is that between A.D. 570 and A.D. 870 seagoing Irish *curraghs* roamed far across the Atlantic, and made landfalls on the American continent.

The next page of history is more clearly written. This is the record of the discovery and attempted colonization of a part of North America called Vinland by Vikings from Greenland in the two centuries or so after about A.D. 986. The story begins in or about that year with a voyage from Iceland to Greenland by a man called Bjarni Herjolfsson, who was a merchant trading between Norway and the Viking settlements in Iceland. Returning to Iceland from Norway, he found that his father had gone off with another Norwegian-Icelander, Eirik the Red (because he had a fine red beard) to establish a colony in Greenland, which had been discovered by Eirik a few years before. Bjarni decided to follow his father, and set off after him. On the way he met bad weather, and was blown far off his course into an area of the sea covered with dense fog. After drifting for several days in fog the weather cleared, and he saw an unknown coast ahead of him. He drew in close to the coast, noted that it seemed pleasant and well-wooded, but, fearing attack by hostile natives, did not go ashore.

Taking bearings from the sun, he realized that he was far to the south of Greenland, so he sailed generally north-east – he could not go north-west because the land was in the way. A few days later he had another glimpse of land – again a wooded coast – but with a fair wind for making north he sailed on past it. In a few more days he made another landfall, this time a harsh shore of rocks and ice. There was nothing to attract him there, the coast did not fit with what he had been able to learn of Greenland, so he put out to sea again. After a few more days at sea he got to Greenland, and succeeded in finding the fjord where his father had settled.

This was in south-west Greenland, in the neighbourhood

of the modern Julianehaab. Here Eirik the Red had established a colony of tough Vikings and their womenfolk, who were able to live quite well by rough farming and fishing. What they did not have, and needed badly, was wood, for their houses, their furniture and their boats (wood to those tenth century Norsemen was as important as steel is to us). Having no good timber in Greenland, they had to make do with such driftwood as the sea brought them, and whatever could be imported. Iceland, which was their nearest neighbour, was itself getting short of timber, which meant importing wood by longer and more hazardous voyages from Norway. The Greenland settlers were, therefore, very interested in Bjarni's story of the well-wooded land he had seen to the south-west.

Eirik the Red grew old, and his son Leif – Leif Eiriksson – succeeded to the leadership of the Greenland colony. Leif was a bold and enterprising young man, and he determined to find the land that Bjarni had seen. About the year A.D. 1001 he fitted out an expedition to re-sail Bjarni's route. He rediscovered Bjarni's three 'lands' and named them – Helluland (Land of Flat Stones) for the rocky icebound shore, Markland (Forest Land) for the next, and Vinland (Wineland) for the pleasantest and most southerly, because he found wild grapes growing there. He wintered there and sailed home the next year, with a valuable cargo of dried grapes and wood.

A few years later – perhaps about the year A.D. 1006-1007 – a friend of Leif's called Thorfinn Karlsefni, who had married the widow of one of Leif's brothers, set out with his wife and a band of other men and women on a colonizing expedition to the newly discovered land. They took farm animals with them and intended to establish a permanent settlement in Leif's 'Vinland'. They found the place where he had wintered, thought it a splendid countryside and set about building homes. They stayed for three years, and Thorfinn's wife, Gudrid, bore a son there. They called the boy Snorri – the first recorded birth of a child of European

Overleaf: This is what a Viking settlement on Vinland might have looked like.

stock in the New World.

Things, however, did not go well with this first settlement. Soon after the settlers had landed some native American Indians appeared, and relations between the newcomers and the Indians quickly became strained. At first the Vikings were greeted with simple curiosity, and goods were exchanged, the Indians trading furs for pieces of red cloth, which particularly attracted them, and for milk, which the Vikings had from their cows and which the Indians, who did not then domesticate cattle, had never met before. But quarrels broke out and the Indians began attacking the settlement. For a time the settlers were able to hold out, but there were many more Indians than settlers, and in the end they decided to give up. Thorfinn and his wife went back to Iceland, where the boy Snorri grew up. But Viking ships went on sailing to North America from Greenland, and there were other settlements, some of which lasted for several generations.

How do we know all this? The voyages of Bjarni Herjolfsson, Leif Eiriksson, Thorfinn Karlsefni and other Vikings from Greenland and Iceland are recorded in a body of literature known as the Icelandic Sagas. These records suffer from the defect of other medieval stories in that they were composed by bards and storytellers for recitation, and not written down until a fairly long time after they were composed. Thus they embody a good deal of folk memory and oral history, which, like the St Brendan literature, is liable to confuse fact with romance. But oral history is not to be despised: even if the Sagas were the only records of the Viking voyages to America, they contain far too much accurate detail to be dismissed as fancy. And they are not the only records. Writing at some date before 1075 in a history of the Archbishopric of Hamburg, in which Greenland and Iceland were then placed, a monk called Adam of Bremen records the discovery of Vinland, and mentions the wild grapes found growing there. This is soon enough after the early Vinland voyages to embody first-hand accounts of them. In 1965 Yale University discovered the so-called 'Vinland Map', copied from a much earlier map around 1440 – half a century before Columbus sailed. This remarkable map shows Greenland in its true position in relation to America, and gives a recognizable outline of the eastern North American coast. More interesting still, an inscription on the map records the visit of a known historical figure, Bishop Eirik Gnupson, as papal legate to Vinland 'in the last year of our most Holy Father Pascal' (Pope Pascal II, who died in 1118). This was over a century after the first Viking settlements in Vinland, so one can say confidently that Norse colonies of some sort must have had a continued existence on the North American continent at least into the twelfth century. Moreover, they must have been quite substantial colonies, for a papal legate is not a missionary priest: he is an important church official, concerned with administration and ecclesiastical diplomacy. Pope Pascal II would not have sent a legate to Vinland unless there were some established Christian community there for him to visit.

The Vinland Map – copied about 1440 from a still unknown original. The Latin caption in the upper left-hand corner records the visit by Bishop Eirik Gnupson to Vinland as Papal Legate.

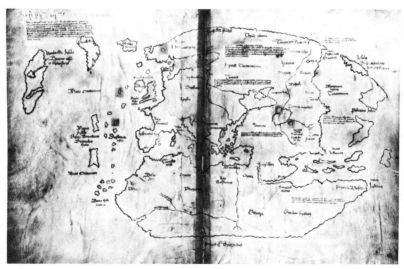

31

But where *was* Vinland? It was certainly in North America, but the Vinland map is in nothing like enough detail to show localities – as far as the map is concerned Vinland might have been anywhere from Labrador to Virginia. By careful study of navigational and other details in the Sagas it is possible to narrow the choice. My own feeling, confirmed by a voyage I made in a sailing boat from Greenland to America in 1966, specifically to try to reconstruct Leif Eiriksson's voyage of 1,000 years before, is that Vinland was in that part of the United States later called New England, probably on the coast of the modern state of Massachusetts. Among the sailing directions in the Sagas is to round a promontory marked by an immense stretch of sand, which the Norsemen called 'Wonder Sands', or 'Marvellous Sands'. This fits Cape Cod and its immense sandy beaches extraordinarily well, and the references to wild grapes and wild wheat fit Massachusetts. The profusion of wild grapes on the shores around Nantucket Sound is still a feature of the place today. There

Despite their superior iron weapons, the greatly outnumbered Vikings were probably

is other evidence that points to New England, one of the most striking bits of it being a piece of anthracite turned up on the site of an old Viking homestead in Greenland which seems to have come from an opencast seam in Rhode Island.

The Norwegian archaeologist, Dr Helge Ingstad, has found the remains of an eleventh or twelfth century Viking settlement in north-eastern Newfoundland, and some people think that this was perhaps where Leif Eiriksson established his first colony. I think it more likely that the Newfoundland settlement was a port of call on the voyage to and from Vinland proper – the climate of Newfoundland does not fit the descriptions of Vinland in the Sagas, and there are other reasons for regarding it as too far north for the main Viking settlements. But the fact that this Viking site has been found in Newfoundland is compelling evidence that Vikings were sailing up and down the eastern seaboard of North America some 350 years before Columbus was born.

The last shadowy reference to Viking-America occurs in

driven out of their colonies by the Indians.

1347, when a ship loaded with timber from Markland (Newfoundland?) and making for Greenland was driven off course in a storm and arrived at Iceland instead. That was nearly 250 years after Leif Eiriksson's first settlement, and if a timber trade with America was going on well into the middle of the fourteenth century, it may be assumed that there were still settlements of some sort to cut and load the timber. What happened to these old Viking settlements? That they were wiped out by the Indians in the end is clear, but why were they destroyed so utterly after lasting for such a long time? Part of the answer can be put in one word – gunpowder. When later European settlers arrived in America they had guns, which gave them an immeasurable superiority in weapons over the Indians, still armed with sticks and stones and bows and arrows. The Vikings had no such superiority, and there were always many more Indians than Vikings. When an Indian was killed, he was quickly replaced by another man from the tribes who lived there. When a Viking was killed he could be replaced only when the next ship arrived from Greenland. And those ships became fewer and fewer, for during the fourteenth century the Viking colonies in Greenland grew weaker and weaker, until in the end they disappeared. Nobody knows exactly what happened to them: one theory is that a ship from Europe brought the plague known as the Black Death, and that so many people died of it that the isolated small communities in Greenland were left too weak to survive. All that can be said is that the Greenland settlements did disappear from history, and the Vinland settlements with them. It is a strange, sad story, but fascinating and exciting, too.

Christopher Columbus

Christopher Columbus, or Christofero Colombo, or Christobal Colon, for he is known by all these names, was born in Genoa in 1451. He went to sea as a boy in Genoese ships trading in the Mediterranean, and later took service with the Portuguese who were making adventurous exploring voyages along the coast of West Africa. Not much is known about his early life. His son, Ferdinand, who wrote a biography of him, says that he visited Iceland, and he may reasonably have told his son about such a voyage; but we have no direct knowledge of it from Columbus himself. The possible link with Iceland, where knowledge of Viking voyages to a new land to the West certainly survived, is at least an interesting one.

Columbus was more than a sailor. He was a gifted navigator, and passionately interested in geography. On his Portuguese voyages to West Africa he noticed something that nobody before him seems to have spotted – the extraordinary persistence of a north-easterly wind in that part of the Atlantic, the wind that later became known as the northeast Trade Wind. Given this wind, he argued, a ship could sail west far more easily than struggle along the Portuguese route to the south. And, since the world is round, a clear run west should bring a vessel to the fabled countries of the east, opening a grand new route by which the gold and spices of the East could be brought to Europe.

It was an exciting idea, for if such a route existed it would bring great riches to any nation which could dominate or control it. But this was still the Middle Ages, and nobody yet knew much about the physical world. It was hard enough to accept that the earth was probably round; if it was, would not some of it be downhill? And even if it was possible to

35

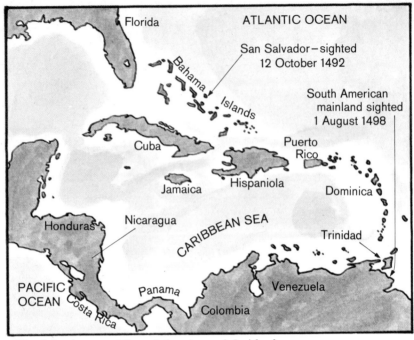

The Atlantic coast of Central America, and the islands.

reach the East by sailing west, the last part of the voyage would be like sailing down a waterfall, and no ship could ever hope to sail up again.

Seamen, knowing how a ship's hull disappears over the horizon before her masts, have always had a better idea of the curvature of the earth than landsmen, but the landsmen were the scholars – and controlled the money. Columbus had no money of his own, so his only hope of fitting out a fleet to make his exploring voyage was to find a wealthy sponsor, which in his day meant a King or Queen. He tried for twelve years – from 1480 to 1492 – offering his scheme to the King of Portugal (John II) and the King of England (Henry VII) before he was able to interest the King and Queen (Ferdinand and Isabella) of Spain. They were joint monarchs, uniting by their marriage the old Kingdoms of Aragon and Castille into one kingdom of Spain. They were enterprising rulers, eager to win for Spain a share of the profitable Atlantic trade (in gold and slaves from West Africa) then being developed by Portugal. So they agreed to back Columbus, fitting out three ships for him in return for nine tenths of the profits of his voyage.

On 3 August 1492 Columbus sailed from Palos, a small town about sixty miles north-west of Cadiz, with three ships. The ratepayers of Palos had to provide two of the ships because they were said to owe money to the Crown. They met this obligation by chartering two small caravels, called the *Pinta* and the *Nina*. The *Pinta* was slightly the larger of the two, about 24 metres (80 feet) long; the *Nina* was about 21 metres (70 feet) long. The King and Queen (or their officials) themselves paid for the third ship, which was to serve as the flagship of the fleet. She was the *Santa Maria*, very little longer than the *Pinta* but rather rounder, and capable of carrying more cargo. She was a type of vessel called a *nao*, designed for the Mediterranean, and nothing like as good a seaboat as the little caravels. *All* these ships were smaller than some of the yachts which took part in the Singlehanded Transatlantic Race in 1972.

The fleet sailed first to Gomera, in the Canary Islands, and departed for their Atlantic crossing on 6 September. Thirty-six days later, on 12 October, they sighted land – the island of San Salvador* in the Bahamas. Columbus landed and took possession of the place for Spain. They sailed on, discovering several more islands, and on 28 October reached Cuba, which Columbus thought was Japan, and part of the mainland of 'India'. The whole of the East was thought of vaguely as 'India', which is why Columbus called the natives of the places he discovered 'Indians', a name which has lasted till today. On this voyage they also discovered Hispaniola (modern Haiti), where the *Santa Maria* was wrecked and became a total loss. Columbus sailed home with the two little caravels, *Pinta* and *Nina*, reaching Lis-

* This, and all other identifications of Columbus's landfalls follow those accepted by Björn Landström, the modern biographer of Columbus, which are much helped by the detailed researches of Admiral Samuel Eliot Morison, the great American naval historian.

The Pinta, *the* Nina *and the* Santa Maria.

·bon on 4 March 1493, and arriving at Palos ten days later.

Still thinking that he had found a route to 'India', Columbus set off on a second transatlantic voyage, this time from Cadiz with a fleet of seventeen ships, on 25 September 1493. He found many more islands, including Jamaica. On this voyage Europeans had their first recorded experience of a West Indian hurricane (called *huracan* in the native Carib language) and several ships were lost. This second voyage lasted for three years. Columbus returned to Spain in 1496, still convinced that Cuba, a huge island some 700 miles long, was part of a mainland continent, though people with him were beginning to have doubts. He made two more transatlantic voyages, 1498–1500 and 1502–04, and it was in 1498 that he first set eyes on the American continent, the coast of Venezuela near the island of Trinidad. On this, his third voyage, he began to realize that he had not found a route to India, but had discovered, as he put it in a dispatch to the King and Queen of Spain, 'another world'. His fourth voyage showed him more of the Caribbean coast of Central America, but he was ill for most of the time and he died (in 1506) some eighteen months after his return to Spain.

Columbus's great voyages, and the quick wealth in gold and jewels that they brought to Spain, making her for a time the greatest power on earth, so changed European and world history that he is commonly regarded as the 'discoverer' of America. This book has shown that he was but one of many 'discoverers' of the New World. This does not lessen his greatness as a seaman and a navigator, but it does put his voyages into a truer perspective. What gives him his unique importance as a discoverer was the *impact* of his discoveries in coming when they did. The Old World was ready to move out of the Middle Ages, Europe was full of new men and new ideas. People were ceasing to be content with the place in society in which they happened to be born. The bright son of a poor family was not prepared to spend his life in humble service to his feudal superiors – he wanted to strike out on his own. Knowledge of an apparently limitless world across the ocean, with land and gold and silver available for the taking, did not just come to Europe – it hit the old, feudal society with the force of an explosion.

But who did this New World belong to?

The idea that it might belong to the people who already lived there scarcely occurred to anyone in the fifteenth cen-

tury. Columbus had made his discoveries in the service of Spain, but Portuguese ships were also exploring in the Atlantic. The governments of Spain and Portugal asked the Pope to divide the world between them, and by the Treaty of Tordesilas (1494) he did just that: he drew an imaginary line from pole to pole passing through a point in the Atlantic calculated at 370 leagues (roughly 1,000 miles) west of the Cape Verde Islands, and decreed that everything to the west of this line should belong to Spain, and everything to the east to Portugal. This audacious division of a still largely undiscovered world between two European nations had little real meaning, and it soon led to trouble with the British, French and Dutch. But it has left its mark on history: the north-east part of Brazil came just within the Portuguese half of the world, so Brazil was colonized from Portugal and not from Spain. That is why the people of Brazil today speak Portuguese while most of their neighbours in South America speak Spanish.

And Columbus himself? His original charter from the King and Queen of Spain made him viceroy of whatever lands he might discover, but although he was a brilliant navigator he was an exceptionally bad colonial governor, and he had to be dismissed. His charter also gave him a one-tenth share of all the revenues from his discoveries, but as men flocked to make their fortunes in his New World this rather vague clause in his agreement became unworkable. He and his family were in fact quite well rewarded by the Spanish government, but he felt that he had been deprived of his rights and died a sadly embittered man.

After Columbus's voyages, discoveries came thick and fast. Although he himself reached the South American mainland (on his third voyage) in August 1498, a wrongly-dated dispatch to the Spanish court suggested that the mainland was first reached by another Spanish captain, Alonso de Hojeda, who was accompanied by a Florentine merchant called Amerigo Vespucci. In fact, Hojeda and Vespucci did not get there until June 1499. As a result of this mistake, Amerigo Vespucci, who wrote about the voyage, was credited with having discovered the new continent, and an early map-maker called it America after his first name. The mistake was discovered, but the name stuck, although the name America may have nothing to do with Amerigo Vespucci at all.

One of Columbus's lieutenants on his first voyage, Vicente Yanez Pinzon, got to Brazil and discovered the River Amazon in 1499 and in 1500 the Portuguese Pedro Alvares Cabral also got to Brazil, making an independent discovery of that great country (which as we have seen, could be claimed by Portugal under the Treaty of Tordesilas). The southern tip of the South American continent was reached in 1520 by the Portuguese navigator Fernao de Magalhaes (Ferdinand Magellan), who discovered the passage leading from the Atlantic to the Pacific that is still called the Magellan Strait. At that time it was thought that Tierra del Fuego and the group of islands, of which Cape Horn is one, at the tip of South America were part of a southern continent reaching to the South Pole. The discovery that there is open sea beyond Cape Horn was made by Sir Francis Drake when he sailed round the world in the *Golden Hind* (1577–81). The first European to reach the Pacific coast of Central America (in 1513) was the Spanish explorer Vasco Nunez de Balboa, whose name is commemorated in the city that stands at the Pacific end of the Panama Canal.

North America Again

While Columbus was busy in the Caribbean, another Genoese seaman, Giovanni Caboto (John Cabot), who had settled in Bristol, determined to look for a sea route to the Indies in the north-west. He obtained a charter from King Henry VII of England entitling him to take possession of any land he might discover on the way, in return for paying 20 per cent of his capital gains to the Crown. It was not a generous charter, for Cabot had to sail at his own expense, but fifteenth-century explorers needed some sort of royal authority for their voyages – otherwise they might be classed as pirates. Practically nothing is known of John Cabot before he came to England. He was about the same age as Columbus – born around 1451 – and had clearly spent much of his life at sea. Unlike Columbus, who had a fleet of three ships for his voyage of 1492, Cabot could raise the money only for one little ship – the *Mathew*, about 50 tons, and slightly smaller than the smallest vessel in Columbus's fleet. Cabot sailed from Bristol in the *Mathew* on 20 May 1497, and on 24 June he discovered a new land, which he called Newfoundland, and took possession of it for King Henry VII. He hurried back to England with the news, and the King gave him £10 for the new land he had added to the British Crown. Next year (1498) Cabot set off with a fleet of five ships to explore his new land more thoroughly. One of these ships had to put back to Bristol soon after the voyage started. The other four, and Cabot with them, were never heard of again.

John Cabot is credited with the 'discovery' of Newfoundland, and it is certainly because of him that other explorers began looking for a north-west passage to India, opening the way to Canada as they did so. But there is fairly good historical evidence that two Icelanders, called Adalbrand

and Thorvald, circumnavigated Newfoundland in 1285, calling it Nyfundnaland (with the same meaning of 'New-found-land'). And there is also evidence of an attempted settlement by a Scandinavian called Landa-Rolf, who is said to have died in Newfoundland in 1295. It is hard to believe that all knowledge of this was lost by 1497 and, since Bristol ships made regular voyages to Iceland for fish, it seems probable that Cabot had a fairly clear idea that there was land to be found where he was going, and even of its name. Cabot may have named America as well as Newfoundland. The collector of customs in Bristol at the time was a certain Richard A'Merryke. He is said to have been one of the financial backers of Cabot's voyage, and it has been suggested that America gets its name from him and not from Amerigo Vespucci.

There was no gold to be had in Newfoundland, but in the seas off Newfoundland and the neighbouring coasts of Labrador and Canada there was wealth in the long run of far greater value than gold – the richest fishing grounds in the world. The Spanish discoveries in Central and South America had all the glamour of gold, but gold was soon spent. The humbler fishermen of Portugal, Britain and France went after the fish. For the next four centuries salt cod from the North American fisheries was one of the staple foods of Europe, and still today (though the fish now is more often refrigerated than salted) these fisheries remain a vital source of Europe's food.

Labrador gets its name from Joas Fernandes, who was a *lavrador*, or smallholder, in the Azores. He got there around 1500–02. By 1504 French fishing vessels sailing from Dieppe had found their way to Newfoundland, and from then onwards fishermen of Normandy, Brittany, the Biscay coast, and the Bristol Channel ports of England and Wales, were regularly crossing the North Atlantic. A Breton from St Malo, Jacques Cartier (1491–1557), was the first to sail up the St Lawrence river to the sites of the modern Quebec and Montreal. Cartier was one of the greatest of French mari-

French fishermen catching cod off the Newfoundland coast.

time explorers, and his three voyages to Canada between
1534–42 put that great country on the modern map. He gave
it the name Canada, probably (Admiral S. E. Morison suggests) from the Canadian-Indian name for a settlement on
the site of what is now Quebec.

The eastern seaboard of what is now the United States
was coasted from Florida to Maine between the years 1524–8
by the Florentine explorer Giovannida Verrazzano (1485–
1528) in the service of the King of France, and further explored by Sir Walter Raleigh (1552–1618), who established
the first English colony in Virginia in 1585. The Arctic coast
of Canada was slowly mapped by a series of fine seamen
seeking the elusive North-West Passage to the Pacific: they
included Sir Martin Frobisher (1539–94), Sir Humfry Gil-
bert (1537–83), John Davis (1543–1605), William Baffin
(1584–1622) and Henry Hudson (d. 1611). Inland, these
Arctic shores were gradually explored by generations of
French and British trappers, seeking valuable furs.

Search for the North-West Passage continued for four
centuries, amassing much geographical knowledge but
always ending in failure to find a sea route through the ice.
Between 1845–8 Sir John Franklin and the entire crews of
two Royal Naval ships (*Erebus* and *Terror*) perished in the
search. A way through from east to west was finally discovered by the Norwegian Roald Amundsen when he sailed

44

the 21-metre (70 feet) sloop *Gjoa* from Greenland to Alaska and on to San Francisco between 1903-06. The Passage was not sailed both ways until 1940-4, when Inspector Henry A. Larsen, of the Canadian Mounted Police, achieved the double voyage in the schooner *St Roch* (equipped with an auxiliary diesel engine).

The Spanish conquerors who followed Columbus to Central and South America, Hernando Cortez (1485-1547) in Mexico, and Francisco Pizarro (1471-1541) in Peru, had ships built to explore the Pacific coast, but until the Panama Canal was opened in 1914 there was no way of sailing from the east to the west coast of either North or South America save by way of Cape Horn (or the Magellan Strait), or by forcing a passage through the Arctic ice. The main routes from Europe to America naturally led to the Atlantic (eastern) seaboard. The Pacific coast of North America remained little known until the eighteenth century voyages of Captain James Cook (1728-79) and his lieutenant George Vancouver (1758-98), after whom the modern city of Vancouver is named.

Roald Amundsen's sloop Gjoa *during the successful navigation of the North-West Passage.*

A Note on Ships

A boat is essentially a framework of ribs, to provide shape and structural strength, planked with some sort of skin to keep out water – it may be planks of wood, skins of animals, canvas, or, in modern times, metal or glass fibre. Reed boats, of the kind in which Thor Heyerdahl believes that ancient peoples crossed from Africa to America have structure and buoyancy combined in the tightly-bound bundles of reed from which they are made; in this respect they may be compared with the modern inflatable rubber dinghy.

The earliest seamen had paddles, oars and sails – all go back to the beginning of seamanship. Early sails were pieces of skin, plaited leaves or bits of cloth held up to help the wind to blow man and boat along – the mast is simply an improvement on standing up to hold a piece of cloth. The first sailors could only sail with the wind – i.e., with the wind more or less directly behind them. As experience was gained with masts and steering oars it was found that boats could still be made to sail with the wind abeam (blowing from the side), and as seamen became still more skilful they were able to sail a little into the wind (with the wind slightly ahead of them). But not much. When the wind was blowing from the wrong direction mariners stayed at anchor (if they could) and waited for it to change; if they were at sea they took off sail and drifted until they could get going again. Oars could help a bit, but were chiefly useful for man-oeuvring inshore – oars, and towing from a dinghy, were the seamen's auxiliaries before engines were invented. Wind was – and is – the sailor's best friend. Columbus's greatest contribution to navigation was his discovery of the North-East Trades and of the complementary Westerlies (whose existence he may have guessed) blowing *from* America *to* Europe in slightly higher latitudes. Out with the Trades, home with the Westerlies was the main road to the New World as long as ships were worked by sail.

The ancient Greeks, Phoenicians, Carthaginians, Arabs and Chinese all had seaworthy wooden ships. The Vikings had splendid ships, though the long rowing boats with

46

shields round them ('longships') that you see in many pictures were warships, not cargo-vessels. The ships in which the Vikings sailed to Vinland were broad in the beam and almost certainly fully decked. (They were able to transport cattle.)

Cooking at sea was done on a brazier standing in a box of sand as a protection against fire. Provisions included sun-dried meat and fish, raisins and other dried fruit, and roasted wheat (flour soon grows mouldy at sea). Water was always a problem, and on long voyages had to be strictly rationed. When rain fell a sail would be rigged to channel it to a water-butt. Such water would often be rather nasty, because a sail, long exposed to salt spray, makes the rain it catches slightly salty.

The North Star (Polaris) has been known from antiquity. It gives direction, and the angle of Polaris, or the angle of the sun at midday, gives a rough indication of latitude – i.e., how far north or south you have gone from where you started. This does not need to be very accurate – early mariners probably took angles with notched sticks or even with their fingers, so many notches or fingers' breadths

(Left) An Italian compass of the sixteenth century. (Right) How to use a quadrant, from The Seaman's Tutor.

means so many miles, or leagues, or whatever they reckoned in. If you know roughly the latitude of a place you have discovered you can get back to it, by sailing north or south until you get to the same latitude, and then going east or west until you get there. This is called 'running down the latitude', and it was the principle of almost all navigation until the invention of the chronometer, enabling accurate time to be kept in the eighteenth century. With an accurate chronometer you can calculate longitude (position east or west on the earth's surface).

A sixteenth-century astrolabe.

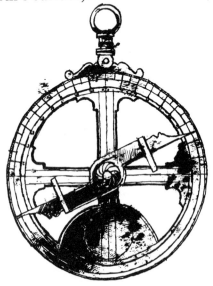

Columbus and all those after him did have compasses, which came into general use during the thirteenth century. These later mariners also had *astrolabes*, graduated discs with moveable pointers, to help them measure angles more accurately.

Above all they had sea-sense – that sixth sense that comes from long experience, enabling men to interpret all sorts of little things – the colour of the sea, the shape of seaweed, the flight of birds, the *feel* of the wind. Courage and sea-sense opened up the world long before instruments were thought of.